Noah's Ark

God saw men killing with
spears and knives.

Greedy women stole food from
each other.

Mean children were cruel to animals.
God was sad that He had made people.

Only Noah and his family were
honest and kind.

God said, "Noah, I am going to send a flood to wash the world clean."
God told Noah what he must do to stay safe.

Noah and his family hammered and sawed,
building a great ark.
Neighbours laughed but they kept working.

When the ark was finished,
Noah gathered the animals inside it.

Noah and his family carried in
sacks of food.

Then the family went into the ark and
God shut the door.
Black clouds gathered and rain began falling.

It rained for forty days and forty nights.

The ark tossed on the waves
as the floodwaters rose higher and higher.

Finally the rain stopped and the ark rested on top of a mountain. Noah sent out a dove to see if the water was going away.

The dove returned with an olive branch.
God sent wind to dry the flood water
while Noah and his family waited.

Then they came out of the ark,
with the animals.

God said, "I promise that I will not send another flood. People and animals will be safe now. I want everything to grow and be healthy.

When it rains, I will set a lovely rainbow
in the sky so you will remember
my promise."